Views
From
Shenir
(Mount of Light)

Cathy Peters Gilot

ISBN 978-1-63844-508-1 (paperback)
ISBN 978-1-63844-509-8 (digital)

Christian Faith Publishing, Inc.
832 Park Avenue
Meadville, PA 16335
www.christianfaithpublishing.com

Printed in the United States of America

Comfort

O God of comfort, God of love,
Feed us with thy Spirit from above,
For you know our hurting heart,
With thy grace, you won't depart,
Fill us ever full and free,
For You know and you see,
Everything we go through, here on earth,
Thou gave Thy Son, through His birth,
God be with us, now we pray,
Guard our heart in Thy perfect way

He Cares

With arms wide open, you can see,
All the plans, I have for thee,
There is no secret from above,
That can surpass My Everlasting Love,
I have come to let you know,
Everywhere that you must go,
Trust Me Now, this very hour,
I have plans within My Power

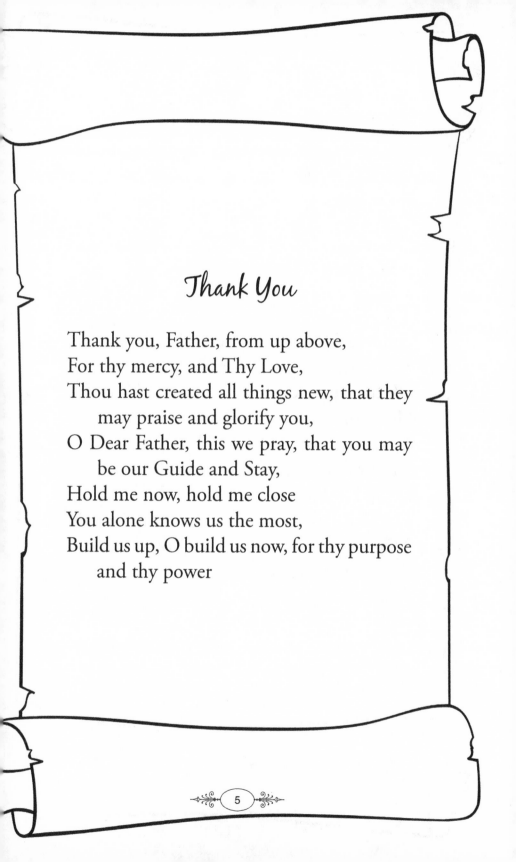

Thank You

Thank you, Father, from up above,
For thy mercy, and Thy Love,
Thou hast created all things new, that they
    may praise and glorify you,
O Dear Father, this we pray, that you may
    be our Guide and Stay,
Hold me now, hold me close
You alone knows us the most,
Build us up, O build us now, for thy purpose
    and thy power

Guide Us

Guide us, Lord, O guide us, be our help
   inside us,
We have waited, Lord, for thee,
Help comes with hearts for Thee,
Mold us, make us in thy Hand,
Until we see the Promised Land,
O God of Heaven, God of earth,
Please still us now and give us joy and mirth,
Thank You, Father, for what you've done,
For your Precious Living Son

To See

Oh, if only we could see ahead,
Of your Awesome and Holy Dread,
We would bow our hearts in prayer,
As we kneel this very hour,
Help us, Father, now we pray
To be steadfast and learn Thy way,
Thou hast helped us, in the past,
With Thy Love, that will ever last

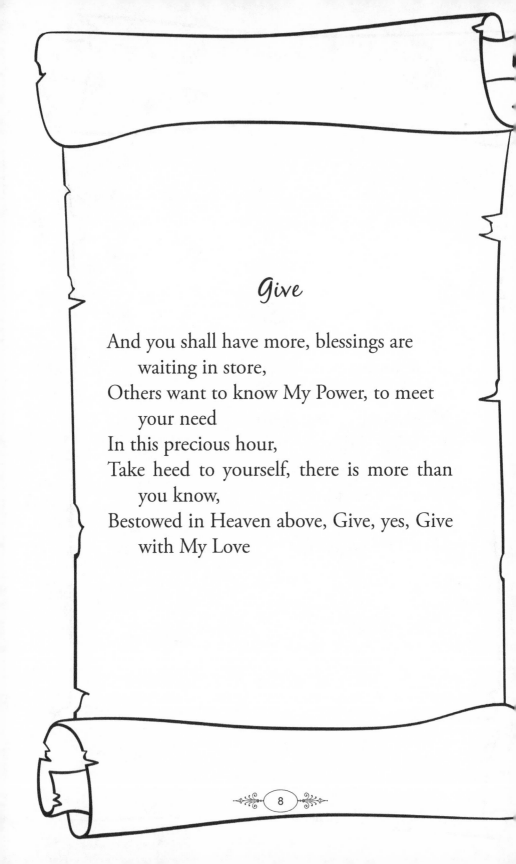

Give

And you shall have more, blessings are
    waiting in store,
Others want to know My Power, to meet
    your need
In this precious hour,
Take heed to yourself, there is more than
    you know,
Bestowed in Heaven above, Give, yes, Give
    with My Love

Waters

Come to the waters full and free,
Come to the waters sent to thee,
Praise Me Now, in this hour,
And you will see, My wondrous power,
Hasten to know My Word of Love,
Given to thee from The Holy Dove

Rest

O that you may rest, yes indeed,
Then you would seek My Face to supply
    thy need,
Be not anxious over much,
But let Me touch thee with My Love,
Look up High, and you will see,
All that you will ever need,
O please Touch, Touch Me now,
In thy hour of need, I will plead,
I know every need and care,
Come to Me and let Me share,
Look to Me up above and be filled with My
    Everlasting Love

Live

Every day with hope anew, there are blessings
    waiting for you,
With My Love, gladly receive, open your
    hand and you will see,
Life anew within My Gates, I will show you
    all the ways,
Hope and Live, Truly Live, take a breath
    and you will see,
So much more that you can be

His Hiding Place

In His secret hiding place, there is a sweet
    fragrance there,
Where all may come to see what He has
    done,
So quiet and peaceful there, is His love
    Shining Near,
To give us what we need, if we will only
    heed,
His Dear Voice, full and free, as our hearts
    are open to see,
Come to this place even now, and you will
    know how,
You can have peace, so sweet, as you kneel
    at Jesus's feet

Kneel

Kneel at Jesus's feet, there that you may Eat,
Of His Grace so fair, He wants to meet you
    there,
Oh, why don't you wait? He'll meet you at
    the Gate,
Of your soul today, Let Him show you the
    way,
Why not Rest and Wait? He'll bring you
    out without a doubt,
So don't try to rush Him, He knows you
    need Him,
To work His Power in you, that He will
    gladly do,
Until you look like Him

Try Me

And you will know, what I have in store for
    thee,
Heed my word, and you will know all the
    plans ordained for
Thee,
Trust my heart, and you will fulfill My Will
    and Purpose for thee,
Know My Ways, and you will have
Everything you need to keep
You safe

Savior

O Blessed Savior, how sweet you are,
He knows what you go through, He's been
    through them too,
He'll show you the way, if you trust in Him
    today,
There is a road ahead, come and rest your
    head,
He'll show you the way,
Trust Him ever and let Him have His way,
Trust in the Lord with all your heart and let
    Him do His part,
He has not left you, let Him guide and keep
    you,
In His Care, you may rest, He will show
    you His very best,
Why not wait right now? He will show you
    how,
Trust Him, yes, trust Him please, He'll
    supply your every need,
He will bring you out, and that's without a
    doubt,
When you do your best, He will do the rest

Blessed

You'll be blessed, when you have stood the
   test,
Don't let your light grow dim, trust only in
   Him,
He will show you the light of Day, when
   you have come His Way,
Try and do your best, come to Jesus and
   rest,
Rest your weary soul, until He has made
   you whole.
On Him you can depend, and on you He
   will send,
All of His Knowledge, Wisdom, and
   Strength,
On Jesus, yes, Christ Jesus you can depend,
Until you have withstood the test, can He
   trust you to the rest,
On Christ Jesus lean on Him your heart,
Trust, yes, trust in Him, He will gladly do
   His part

Star

A star is born along the shore, O look and
    see, I'll show thee more,
The sand so white, the sky so blue, I came
    to look and I saw you,
O hasten not to go away, the setting is for
    you This Day,
O bless Me Now, I know the way, to make
    your heart rejoice and stay

You

You can be free, if you would only seek me,
Not thyself or your emotions, look to Me, I
    am your Portion,
O look to Me and you will stay Free,
Be not bound with fear nor hate, I Am at
    every Gate,
To give you peace and freedom too, to live
    your life ever so New,
Never mind about the past, I Am Here with
    you, and I Will Last

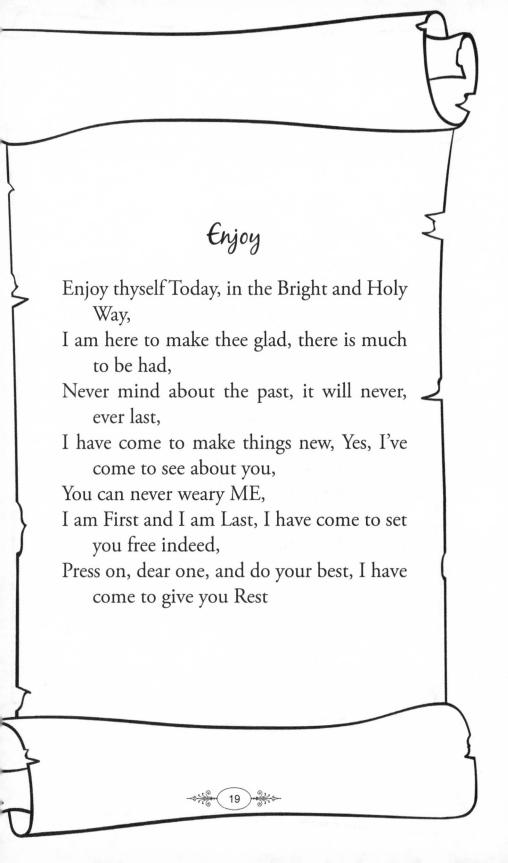

Enjoy

Enjoy thyself Today, in the Bright and Holy
    Way,

I am here to make thee glad, there is much
    to be had,

Never mind about the past, it will never,
    ever last,

I have come to make things new, Yes, I've
    come to see about you,

You can never weary ME,

I am First and I am Last, I have come to set
    you free indeed,

Press on, dear one, and do your best, I have
    come to give you Rest

He May

O perhaps you have wondered along the way,
Why things sometimes don't go your way,
He said in His Word, It's My Choice,
I make all things new, it's My Voice,
So hold on to what He has given to you,
Let it not go untouched,
He'll bring you out, as He has said,
Give us Lord, our Daily Bread

Just He

Just He alone can give our direction in
which we can Live,
Please hope upon His Grace, He alone is in
this place,
Please believe, it is true, He died to Save
even you,
Please believe and you will see, it is Christ,
yes, IT is HE

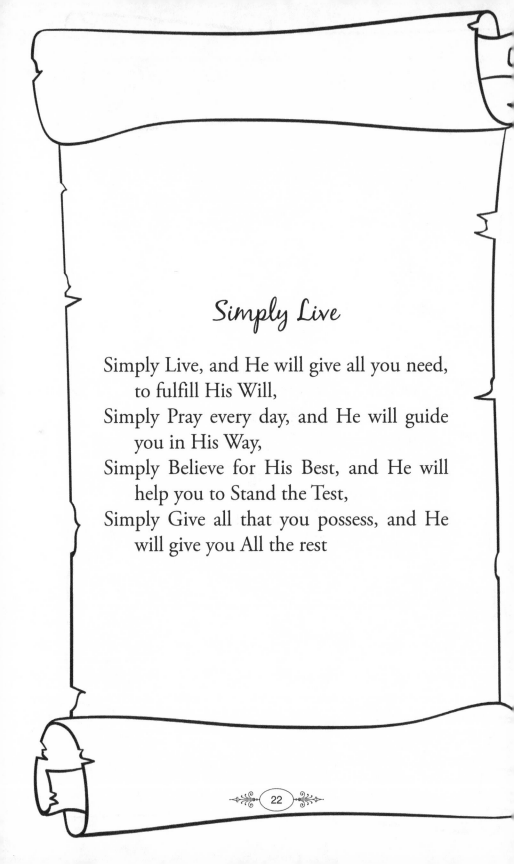

Simply Live

Simply Live, and He will give all you need,
to fulfill His Will,
Simply Pray every day, and He will guide
you in His Way,
Simply Believe for His Best, and He will
help you to Stand the Test,
Simply Give all that you possess, and He
will give you All the rest

I Am He

Who died for thee, I am He who will raise
　　thee to see,
All the wonders of My Love, sent to thee
　　from up above,
Do not fear to take unto thee, all the
　　blessings I have for thee,
Hasten, yes, hasten to My Love, sent to thee
　　from up above

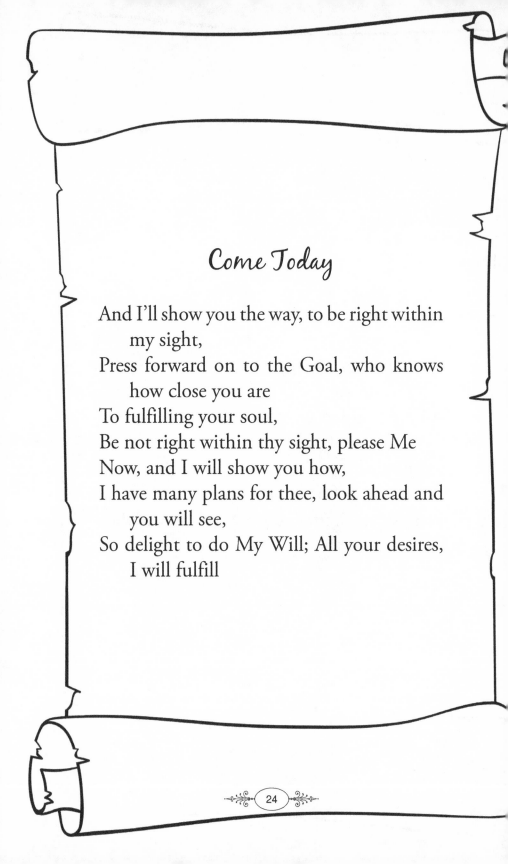

Come Today

And I'll show you the way, to be right within
    my sight,
Press forward on to the Goal, who knows
    how close you are
To fulfilling your soul,
Be not right within thy sight, please Me
Now, and I will show you how,
I have many plans for thee, look ahead and
    you will see,
So delight to do My Will; All your desires,
    I will fulfill

Near You

O Heavenly Father from up above,
To be near You is Great Love,
Hold my hand in this hour,
Let me stand with Thy Power,
May thy Grace and Sweet Communion,
Hold us near in this Heavenly Union,
Never let us go astray,
You, we need from Day to Day,
Seek us with Thy mighty Love,
Shine on us from Up Above

Stay

Stay beneath the Cross of Christ; Let Its
    Shadow guide thy life,
To new heights far up Above, always waiting
    to show My Love,
Be not hasty to go Thy way, My Way is best,
    and please do stay,
You will be glad you did, in My Realm are
    blessings Hid,
I Am He that knows The Way, I will guide
    thee from Day to Day,
O please wait, there is more, you My Child,
    I Love and Adore,
Let me shield thee from Thy Past, My Love
    for thee will Always Last,
Never seek another way, I Am Thy Guide,
    and Yes, Do Stay

Love

Love is new every day, I will show you My
  Precious Way,
To be free of things that bind, I Am He—
  My Love is Kind,
Gentle to last always and to brighten and
  fill your ways,
With the best I have for you, seek My Love,
  it is Appointed and always True,
Lift your eyes up above, and please receive
  My Everlasting Love,
Love Gives and Shields the things so
  precious,
Till its reflection is seen, Entirely Gracious,
Let Me Love You as I please, and you will
  know I Am He that sees your needs,
Call upon My Name, ever often, know My
  Heart that you're Never Forgotten

Hear

Hear Me Now, and I will Speak, come near
    now, and bow at My Feet,
Open thy heart and Receive, All I have, and
    do give heed,
Rest in my Constant Care, Hear My Voice
    for I Am There,
Ever so Quiet, I will Speak, be patient and
    listen, and Always take heed,
To My Voice, so Clear and Sweet, is thy
    desires I long to meet,
Hasten now, I'll show you the Way, to
    brighten your path, and heed My Way

Help

I will help you did You know? Just only ask
    Me, and I will show,
All the ways of Mine you see, are ever
    designed to Hear thy plea,
O Rest, please Rest and seek Me First, I will
    gladly quench thy thirst,
No one else, but only Me, can ever help you
    as you need,
Come to Me with all your heart, let Me do
    My Blessed Part,
I will lift you up, and you will see, it is I
    who can only Plead,
Trust Me only, I Am the Way, seek not to
    go astray,
I have you already, in My Everlasting Arms,
Let Me Hold and Keep you from All alarms

Taken

By the Blood of Jesus, just to make me
 whole,
Just to forgive me for my sins and to save
 my sin sick soul,
Oh, won't you come with me? To this
 Blessed Fountain of Life?
For He Gave His Only Begotten Son, so
 that we might Live,
And serve Him right,
O don't you hear His Dear voice pleading?
Won't you come to Him Today?
He wants to take you in His Great Arms,
 and show you The way

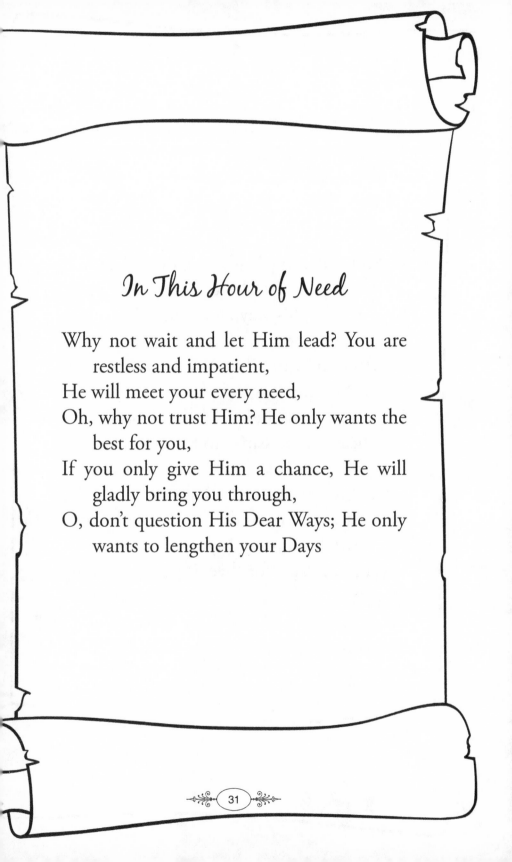

In This Hour of Need

Why not wait and let Him lead? You are
    restless and impatient,
He will meet your every need,
Oh, why not trust Him? He only wants the
    best for you,
If you only give Him a chance, He will
    gladly bring you through,
O, don't question His Dear Ways; He only
    wants to lengthen your Days

Be Still

Be Still and know My Voice, Be Still and I'll
make you My Choice,
I have come this way alone, now I sit upon
My Throne,
You too can know The Way, if you seek to
Be Still this day,
Come on now and don't hold back, just
ahead are Blessings to fill thy lack,
Look not back, just look ahead, I have come
to give to you your Daily Bread,
So trust Me Now to do My Best, lean your
weary head upon My Breast,
Yes, I have Plans for thee, if you could only
See,
Please believe and stand the Test, I will do
to you my very Best

Come Now

The hour is late, you must hasten into My
    Gates,
Life anew waits for thee, this is My earnest
    plea,
Pray and stand before Me now, I will gladly
    show you how,
Come closer, don't linger back, now is the
    time to behold and don't slack,
Say goodbye to the world below, I will show
    you worlds untold,
I desire to fill your soul, with untold riches
    of Mine until you overflow,
Up, up High is My Grace, seek to know My
    Unfailing Place,
If you stand with Me this hour, you will
    know My Never Failing Power

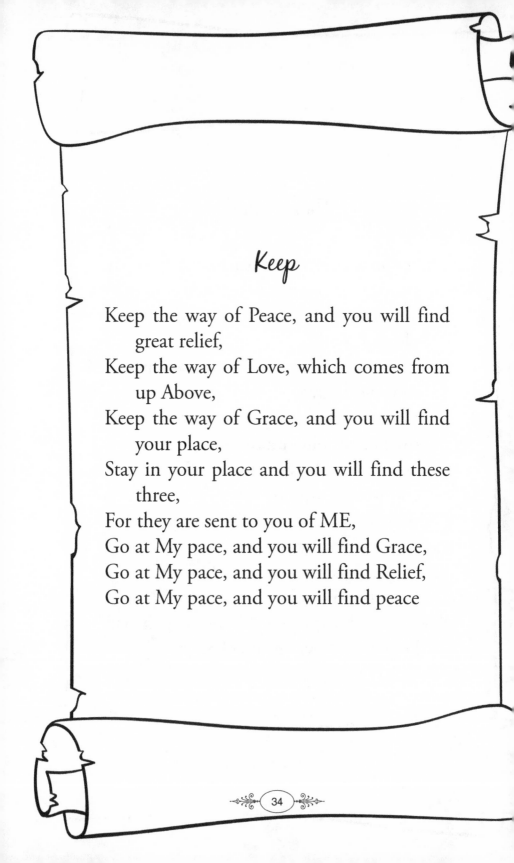

Keep

Keep the way of Peace, and you will find
    great relief,
Keep the way of Love, which comes from
    up Above,
Keep the way of Grace, and you will find
    your place,
Stay in your place and you will find these
    three,
For they are sent to you of ME,
Go at My pace, and you will find Grace,
Go at My pace, and you will find Relief,
Go at My pace, and you will find peace

Close

Close the door to doubt and fear, and you
will hear a song,
Of cheer ringing in your ears,
Close the door to hate, and you will stand
at My Gates,
Close the door to lack, and you will have
more to give to others,
Close the door to darkness, and you will
live in My Light Above,
Open the door to Love, and you will sing
anew,
For it was created just for you,
Open the door to Faith, and I will make
you great
Open the door to Peace, and you will find
great release,
Keep the door of your heart open to ME

Wealth

Wealth and Riches are yours untold,
As you come to the Father of Love,
Lean on My Breast, I will make thee whole,
As you stay within My Fold,
Pure and Sweet is My Love for thee,
O why not hasten, come and see,
Come to the Waters from up Above,
There I will show thee My Great Love,
Seek to know Me, as I already know,
And see thee,
Great is My Power unto you this hour,
Come and stay with Me Today,
I will lead and guide you in My Way

O Dwell with Me

And you will see, all the plans I have for thee,
O trust in Me, and you will know,
My will for thee, for thou must go,
O see in Me My Light Shining clear,
As I whisper My Love within thy ear,
O Bow thy head and hear, the sweet drops
 of rain,
Coming down from Above, from the Father
 of Love,
O test Me now and know My ways,
And long shall be thy very days
I am He that calls thee,
Seek My Face and know My Grace,
Come out to Me, and shout a Praise,
And you will seek and know all My Ways,
Be Not weary, come and see, All My Plans I
 have for thee

A Song

The sweetest Song you'll ever hear,
Is the song that says, that Christ is Near,
There is no brighter hope so clear,
Ringing so loud within your ear,
Of harps of Joy, and bells of Cheer,
Because Jesus Is Near

Hope

Hope in Me is never lost,
When you know the one who paid the Cost,
Don't despair when you can't see,
Hope in God who will set you free,
I have come to give you Rest,
Only trust Me and do you best,
I know you and what lies ahead,
Come unto Me, and do not dread,
I Am He who's gone ahead,
And Please trust Me, and raise your head,
Look to the skies where Hope is born,
I am waiting to give you your Corn (Bread
    of Life)

Be True

Please be true to the voice you hear,
Hoping to bring you ever so near,
Do not balk and turn your back,
You will only suffer lack,
Draw near please with a true heart,
And let Me do My gracious part,
Never question or dismay,
I Am He who creates each New day

Peace

Peace is yours to have and to hold,
Seek Me first for riches untold,
Be quiet and still, and you will see,
Peace was sent to you to feel,
Sometimes troubles come and go,
Always seek Peace, and don't let go,
Peace is real, so settle down,
Let in your mind and soul,
Your Holy Crown

More

Seek to know Me more, I Am waiting at the
    door,
Of your heart you'll see, more of Me for thee,
Do not question what you cannot see,
Just come to Me and keep believing,
I have reserved for you the Best
Please be still and stand the test,
Not much longer is the time,
I Am yours, and you are mine,
Seek not to know before the time,
I will cause thy face to shine,
Joy and Peace and love anew,
I have waiting to give to you,
I Am at your heart's door,
Come to Me, and I'll give you more

Pray

Others are waiting around the world,
    breathlessly waiting to be heard,
Intercede thy very best, for them also to
    stand the test,
They can feel when you are real, Prayer
    travels far and has its Wings,
Don't be weary in your quest, trust God
    only to do what's best

Trust

Trust in Me, I know the way, and I will turn
　　your midnight into day,
Pray, Trust, Live, and Give, this is the Day
　　that you shall live,
Look not back, nor seek the bad, just ahead
　　is all you ever had,
I know what's best for you, trust Me now to
　　bring it through,
Hold on a little while longer so that your
　　soul will never hunger,
I have brought you safe thus far, and I will
　　lead you on tomorrow,
Safely rest within my will, and My Best, I'll
　　gladly give,
Satan's power can never keep from you what
　　I have planned for you,
Don't give up or be afraid, this is the day
　　that I have made,

Mine

You are mine, and I am yours, I will open
  up all the Doors,
Where you must enter, and you will see, all
  that you will ever need,
Choose the best, stand the test, I AM He
  that undergirds thee,
Walk in my steps and keep my Word, all
  your prayers are surely heard,
Don't be doubtful, keep on pressing, there
  is Sure Joy and ever Blessing,
Lean on Me, I don't mind, I Am yours, and
  you are mine

Just

Just when you think you cannot take
    anymore,
There opens up a Bright New Door,
Filled with Newness you never knew before,
Leading you to A brand-New Shore,
Do not stop just yet, there is more, yes,
    more up ahead,
Please keep looking and hoping to see,
More of Me to fill your days,
I know you're tired of traveling so fast,
I have strength anew to help you last,
Look up into My Face Above, and I will fill
    you with My Love,
Do not falter or fear to trust me, I only want
    to bless and keep thee,

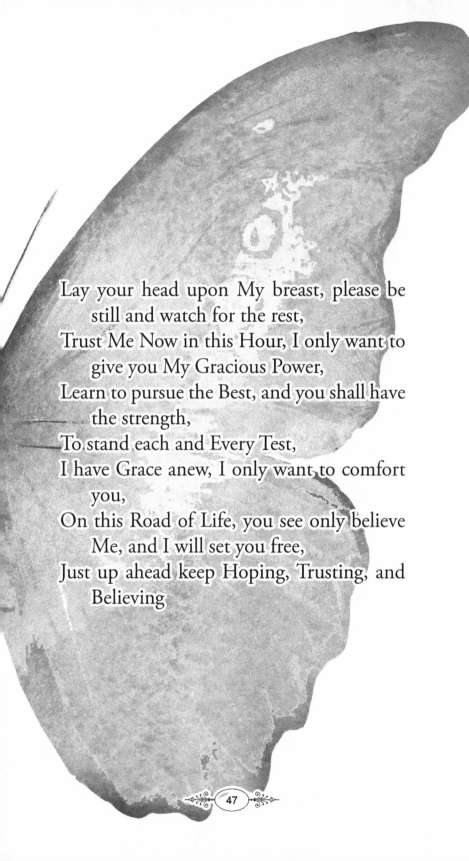

Lay your head upon My breast, please be
    still and watch for the rest,
Trust Me Now in this Hour, I only want to
    give you My Gracious Power,
Learn to pursue the Best, and you shall have
    the strength,
To stand each and Every Test,
I have Grace anew, I only want to comfort
    you,
On this Road of Life, you see only believe
    Me, and I will set you free,
Just up ahead keep Hoping, Trusting, and
    Believing

The Robe of Righteousness

The robe He wore must have borne,
No signs of Life, but sin and strife,
While they cast lots for it,
Not knowing Jesus's power was all over it,
He wore it to symbolize, His great love for us,
To cover our sins, with His Ever Life-Giving
    Blood
O think of His power in that Life-Giving
    Hour,
Who did no wrong, but now sits on His
    Throne,
O do not forget Him, His cry was heard,
Around the world, as Satan's darts at Him
    were hurled,

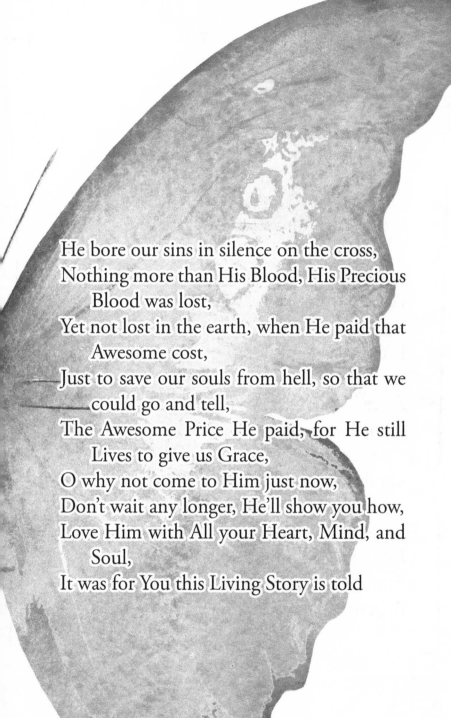

He bore our sins in silence on the cross,
Nothing more than His Blood, His Precious
    Blood was lost,
Yet not lost in the earth, when He paid that
    Awesome cost,
Just to save our souls from hell, so that we
    could go and tell,
The Awesome Price He paid, for He still
    Lives to give us Grace,
O why not come to Him just now,
Don't wait any longer, He'll show you how,
Love Him with All your Heart, Mind, and
    Soul,
It was for You this Living Story is told

Mind

Keep your mind stayed on Me, and I will
    set you free,
Trust in Me Now, and you know how,
Peace of mind, please seek, it is prepared
    for the meek,
I Am Meek and Lowly in Heart, let Me Do
    My Part,
Peace like a River, you can have,
If you'll only let Me keep your mind stayed
    on Me,
Let the Mind of Christ dwell in you Richly,
Through My Precious Word I have given thee,
Care not for the things of the world,
Keep your mind focused on Me,
And I will keep thee in Perfect Peace,
Believe Me Now, I know How

Depend

Depend on Me, and I will set you free,
Stop trusting in yourself, you will continue
    to fail,
Don't depend on things, they will not last,
Forget about the past, I Am Here to Last,
Empty your heart to Me, and I will set you
    free,
I know what's best, please endure This Test,
I know you are tired, there is Everlasting
    Strength in Me,
For you are My hired,
Hold on to Me now, and don't let go for a
    moment,
In the hour you think not, that's when I'm
    still There,
Holding your Hand, as you travel through
    this land,
I will set you free, as you continue to believe
    in ME

Grace

O this Grace so sweet, is waiting for you to
    see,
Just as Christ is King, so shall your soul sing,
Preciously given to us Who did not deserve it,
Redeemed from the curse of sin,
To have overflowing joy within,
Please come and enjoy, this wondrous Gift
    so free

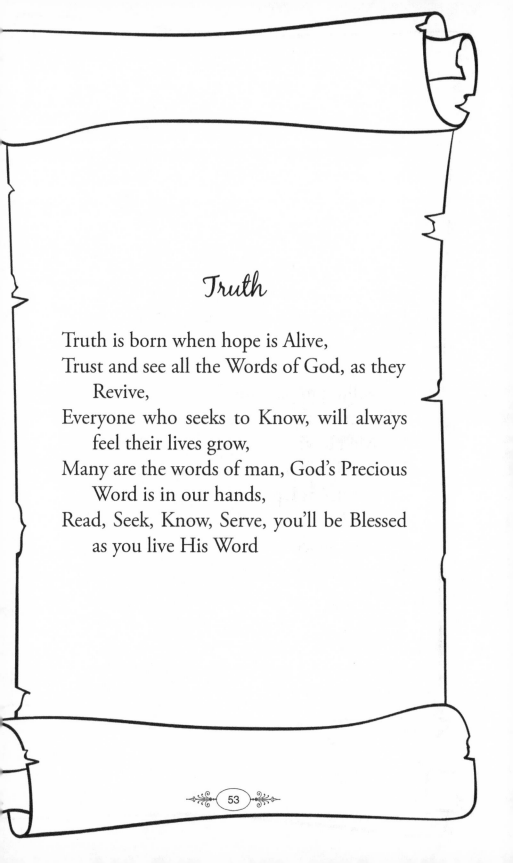

Truth

Truth is born when hope is Alive,
Trust and see all the Words of God, as they
   Revive,
Everyone who seeks to Know, will always
   feel their lives grow,
Many are the words of man, God's Precious
   Word is in our hands,
Read, Seek, Know, Serve, you'll be Blessed
   as you live His Word

More

I came to give you more, as you stand
    waiting at My Door,
Hope in Me is never Lost, as when you're
    willing to pay the Cost,
Will you not come to Me now? Cease to ask
    Me How?
I have Plans you know not of, sent only to
    you from Up Above,
So Test Me Now, in this hour, and you shall
    experience my
Wondrous Holy Power

Soon

There will be a time, when sorrows are ceased,
When tears are dried, when Joy is increased,
Don't be afraid to live the Life you were given,
Your Heavenly Father knows just how much
more in you is risen,
To accept the best only is not enough,
We must embrace it all, if we want to be tough,
Go on your way singing in your heart,
God is aware of the stops and the starts,
He wants to make of you His Best,
Lean your weary head upon His Tender
Loving Breast

Someday

You will be glad you went through, even
though sometimes,
You complained silently or loudly to others,
Be still Now and know that God's will is
always best,
He will always help you to stand the test,
In His own time and not yours, you'll rejoice
because,
You have finished your course,
Look Up Above and realize that the end is
near,
And will not return back
Rejoice and be glad in the Lord,
He holds the future as well as the past,
His Plans for you will always last

Failed

You may have failed yourself and others,
But God and His Precious Word never fails,
He will give you the strength to last,
If you will only let go of the past,
Up Above is His Love waiting and ready to
Pour it into your heart and soul,
So that you can be made perfectly whole,
Rejoice and look up, see the wonderful
Blessings He has prepared for thee,
Sing unto Him with all your might,
God will cause everything to turn out all right,
He has gone this Way before,
Only through Jesus Christ is the Door,
Hold on to your Hope anew,
He wants only to fix it for you,
Trust Him with your life,
Only God is the Perfect and True Light

Way

Way back on Calvary, Jesus died for you
   and me,
He is the Door, the Life, and the Way,
If we would only trust Him day by day,
He died to Save us from our sins,
Come, yes, come to Him and you will win,
In this life, there is darkness and trouble,
Look unto Jesus, and your joy will double,
He alone can save your soul,
He alone can make you whole,
Why look back on things of the past?
Look ahead to precious blessings that last,
He can truly set you free, only believe Him,
And you will see,
He alone knows what's best for you,
You're made in His Image and He will take
   you through

Rain

Let God Rain in your soul, abundance of
Blessings to make and unfold,
His Word of Love in your soul,
Blessed are they that Keep His Word,
Ever coming from the God of Love,
Giving Life ever anew, to everyone and even
  you,
Be True and let it, The Word, overflow you

Trust Me

I Am the Way, I will lead and guide you
from day to day,
Look at My Hands, they are open, to show
you I care
And give you what you're hoping,
Stand clear and see all the Blessings planned
for thee,
Trust Me Now and come closer, I will shield
thee
From All that happens

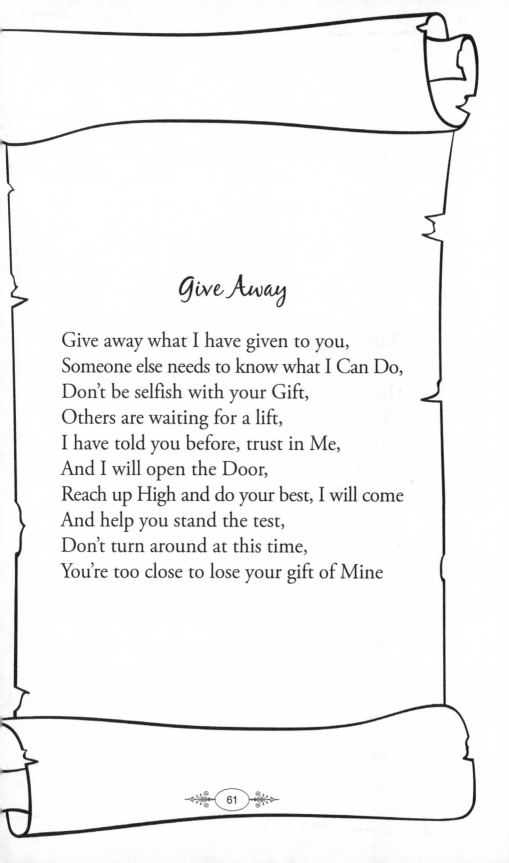

Give Away

Give away what I have given to you,
Someone else needs to know what I Can Do,
Don't be selfish with your Gift,
Others are waiting for a lift,
I have told you before, trust in Me,
And I will open the Door,
Reach up High and do your best, I will come
And help you stand the test,
Don't turn around at this time,
You're too close to lose your gift of Mine

Triumph

Triumph upon the High Places set for thee,
I will Heal you, and set you free,
Then you shall know that it is I, whose Throne
Is in Heaven, but yet very nigh,
Question not, nor look back, it was meant for
Thee to have No lack,
Yes, it's been long and hard, don't give up
   your Faith,
And Never discard

Gone

Gone are the days of sadness and
disappointments,
Look to bright Days ahead for you,
Do not follow me at length, Do, come closer
to Me, and Stay,
Look for your blessings which are near to
come,
Don't forget to include others in your
prayers

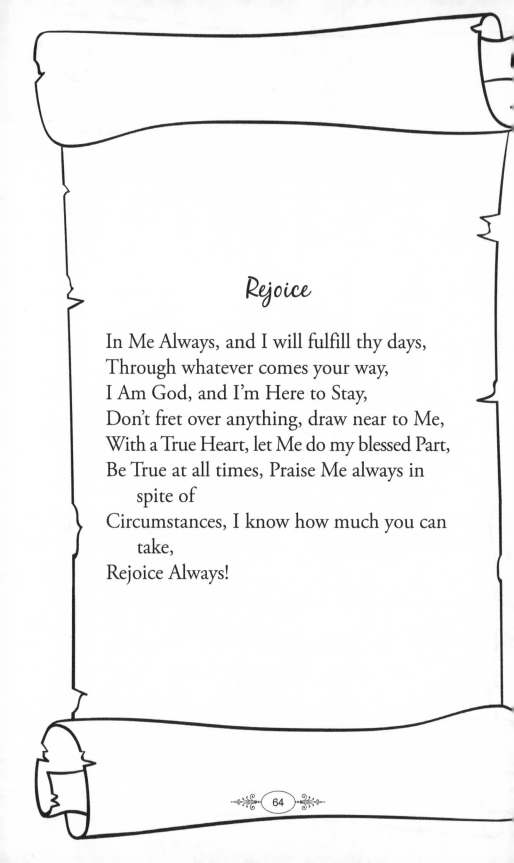

Rejoice

In Me Always, and I will fulfill thy days,
Through whatever comes your way,
I Am God, and I'm Here to Stay,
Don't fret over anything, draw near to Me,
With a True Heart, let Me do my blessed Part,
Be True at all times, Praise Me always in
    spite of
Circumstances, I know how much you can
    take,
Rejoice Always!

Seek Me

Forget about yourself, I know what's best,
Even when you stand the test,
Wait on Me, I Am Here, just be still,
Take My Hand, I am near,
Never fret, I know what's best, when you are
Ready, I'll lead and guide you to My Best,
Take what has been given you,
I am your Father, and I'll bring you through

Stand By Me

And you will know, all the Paths that I will
Cause you to grow,
Look Above and you will see, it is I who
Loves and Cares for thee,
Don't try to understand until you have
Tried My Hand,
All that hurts is best to learn, many ways
Of Life to cause you not to spurn,
Come on forward now, I will teach
You, and you'll know how,
Be not troubled over what you may lose,
I Am the One that you must Choose,
Learn to pass the test at hand,
Seek to stay in the pleasant land,
I have not forgotten you, look ahead
There's Light Anew

When Hope Is Born

The Sky is bluer, the Clouds are lighter,
The Grass is greener, the Sun Shines
    Brighter,
Your heart begins to Sing, God's Love flows,
And wells up in your soul, you feel as though
You could hug everyone you see,
The Birds' sweet singing is heard so much
    clearer,
Although these earthly and heavenly
    thoughts
Take over; there is nothing quite so precious as
The Words of God expressed through
    Solomon
In Chapter 2:10–13

Cheer

Cheer Up, Cheer Up my Son,
Your God is near you right now,
Why faint or fear, when your God
Is near you, I have come to lift you up,
Not to cast you down,
Let go the cares of this Life,
They will only wound and grieve you,
Be of Good Cheer
For thy God is Near

Dare To Dream

Of things above, of My Mercy and My Love,
I have come to Comfort you and to Bless
    and bring you through,
Look not to things below, they will cease to
    let you grow,
Be of Good Cheer, look Above, there you
    will find Mercy and Great Love

Tender

Tender are the arms of God, holding you so
    close,
Tender is His Love for you, in this you can
    boast,
All is gone of the old, old heart, He wants
    to entrust,
To you, of a brand-new Start,
Hear His voice speaking now, ever so soft
    and clear,
Know He is right beside you, whispering in
    your ear

Wait

Is the key to All blessings, it may seem hard;
But it is in listening, hearing from Me,
I know you've come this far, Wait some more
For good things to fill your heart,
Why question when I Am El Shaddai?
I Made you in My own Image,
Trust your Body to Me

Song

Sing to Me a New Song, come to Me with
    rejoicing,
Open your heart to Life, Love, Hope, and
    Joy,
Refuse to live in the past, look forward to
    what will Last,
Be Still

Poor

Poor is he who comes to Me, I alone can set
you free,

Humble yourself and look Above, ever seek
My Everlasting Love,

Cast your cares and never doubt, I alone
will bring you out,

Come, yes, come with all your heart, I'll
take you forward,

And give you a new start

Troubles

Don't last always, God Above knows our days,
He will come and bless when we have
    withstood His Test,
Don't cry and weep or mourn, for our own
    sins has
Jesus, God's Son already born,
God knows the way we take, He is ever with
    us always,
So look up and take heart, He has been with
    us from the start,
Ever lean on Him and be strong, He can
    never do No Wrong,
At the end of the day, you will arise and give
    Him All the Praise

Just for Today

I come to thee, to store My Love in thee
from Up Above,
Stay with Me and see, all that is planned for
thee,
Look up! I Am Here to stay close to thee,
I will help you to stand, just be faithful and
hold My hand,
Look to Me and give Me your heart, I Am
all you need to succeed,
In the way that I shall lead

Sure

Be sure of the things you see, for they are
   sent to you from me,
Judge not the outer appearance, but be still
   and you will see,
The inner substance,
Stand tall and look ahead, there are many
   things to see instead,
Do not doubt at any time, I Am yours and
   you are mine,

Might

In My Might move ahead,
Never mind what is dead,
Step over the past mistakes,
In My Might, you'll have what it takes,
Look at Me and follow close,
You need Me Now, I Am, The Most

Faith

Faith is best when it is tested,
Lean on Me and you can be rested,
Never mind what comes to test,
Think on Me and do your best,
Wait, yes, wait a little longer,
Knowing in Me only, you can become
    stronger,
Faith gives light to those who believe,
Trust in Me and you shall receive,
Dark may be the road ahead,
Lean totally on Me and rest your head

Steps

Steps of faith lead higher and higher,
So that you can have more power,
Look above and see My Light,
In My realm, you shall have much might,
Round and round that you may go,
Often causes you to grow, I Am with you now,
Take My Hand and I'll show you How

Look

Look to the hills which comes your help,
Step up and see what lies ahead,
Keep your sight off things below,
Fulfill your purpose and let it show,
I Am He who will help you until,
My Perfect Will for you is fulfilled,
Never mind what others may or may not
    think,
I Am your God, I AM HE

Test

You must stand the test,
When you've tried your best,
Little do you know,
That there's still more room to grow,
Cease to measure yourself,
By others successes,
I Am the Way, and I will guide your days,
Trust Me Now you see, I Am Jesus, I AM HE

Quiet

Be quiet, be quiet, Open your ears,
The Voice of quietness is very near,
Seek to rest and be still,
Enjoy being quiet, you will be strengthened
    within,
Seek not to press against My Will,
Be quiet, yes, quiet and only Sit Still

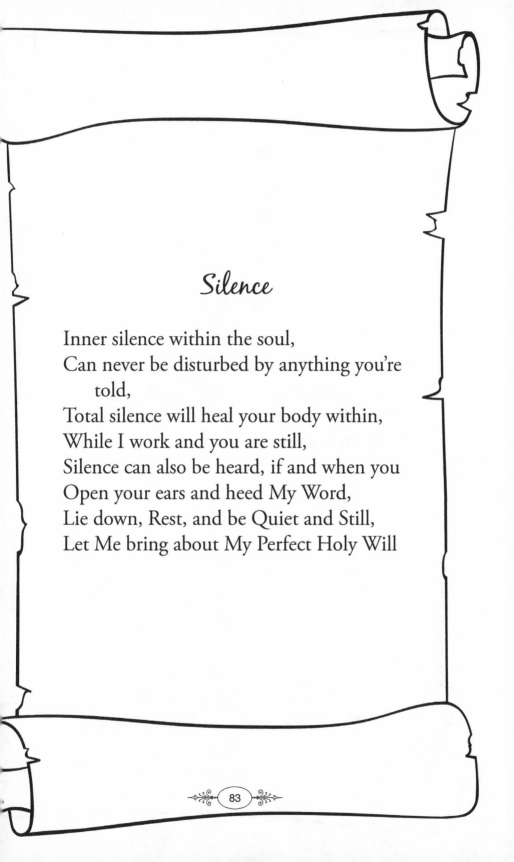

Silence

Inner silence within the soul,
Can never be disturbed by anything you're
    told,
Total silence will heal your body within,
While I work and you are still,
Silence can also be heard, if and when you
Open your ears and heed My Word,
Lie down, Rest, and be Quiet and Still,
Let Me bring about My Perfect Holy Will

Holy

I only, I Am Holy and Mighty,
I can do Anything and still Sit Highly,
Upon My Throne are riches untold,
Come near in Prayer, and let me unfold,
Righteousness, Holiness, Faith, and Cheer,
I Am ever, ever so Near,
Yes, I long to give you Power,
Only let go and come near this very Hour

Come Forth

Yes, please come forth out of your past,
Let go of all cares; they will and shall not last,
Walk within My Path ahead,
Raise up your eyes and eat only, My Bread
   (WORD)
Until you are full and running over,
Only then can you be a Blessing to others,
Stop looking back, the Time is short,
I Am He who will bring you forth,
Come on Now, I have a Token,
And the key to your heart, so please keep it
   Open

Fair

Fair days are ahead, and I Am the Way
Come near to Me Now, and please, please
    do stay,
Look up High and be Strong,
Look to the hills and sing a New Song,
Be not shaken concerning what others may
    or may not do,
I have come to set you free, yes even you,
I have given you My Holy Power to Stand
    Each Test,
Look up to Me, and do your very best

Keep

Keep My Law and Look Above,
There up High is only LOVE,
Along with Faith and Righteousness anew,
It is yours, and I will give it to you,
Hold, yes, hold on to the Things that last,
Ever, even Now let go your past,
Live in the present, do and finish My Work,
Given to you; Yes, stay in the New

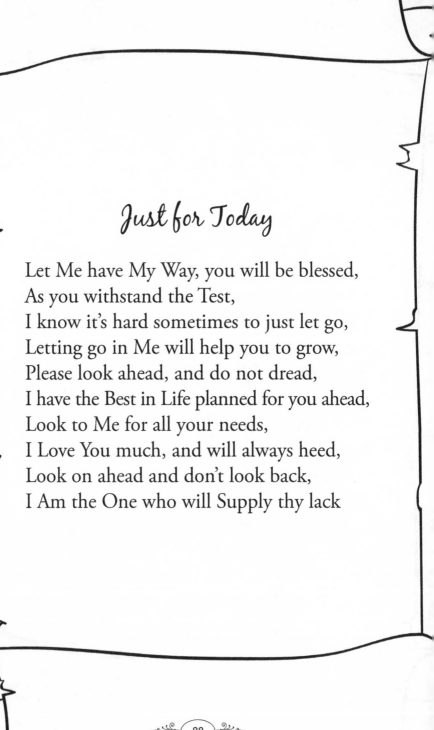

Just for Today

Let Me have My Way, you will be blessed,
As you withstand the Test,
I know it's hard sometimes to just let go,
Letting go in Me will help you to grow,
Please look ahead, and do not dread,
I have the Best in Life planned for you ahead,
Look to Me for all your needs,
I Love You much, and will always heed,
Look on ahead and don't look back,
I Am the One who will Supply thy lack

Pure

Pure is the Word of God, Holy is His Name,
Keep on trusting in Him, He is always the
    same,
White as the driven snow, so close is His Heart,
He wants to share with you every single part,
Come closer Now, all you want to know,
Just look up to Him, and why not Now,
Closer to His Heart, and He'll impart,
All Pureness and Cleanness throughout
    your soul His Part

Start

Start to make a change, call upon My Name,
I Am near you know, I want to see you grow,
More and more each day, until you see My
    Way,
Close to My Heart, Please Come, until you
    can see it's done,
All that you desire, I will bring you higher,
Lean on Me, Please Lean, until I have made
    you clean,
Others will see and know, I have made you
    to grow,
Look up High and see, All I have for thee

Grow

Grow up in God and know the paths that
    you must go,
Don't be afraid to ask Me for directions that
    will last,
Seek to know My Face, and I will give you
    added Grace,
For each challenge of the day, you will learn
    to know My Ways,
The Pathway is not hard, let your Faith be
    you Guard,
Against the things of the past, that will
    never, never last

Open

Up to me, and I will set you free,
Don't remain closed to what you could be
    enjoying now,
Stay close and seek more, I'm willing to
    show you how,
Humble yourself before me and stay still,
Until you discover My Perfect Will,
Don't question in your mind, I Am yours
    and you are mine

How Important It Is to Obey

How sweet to walk in His Way
Listening for His Voice every day,
Through trials great, through trials small,
Letting Him be your All and All,
Knowing Him makes your life so Bright,
Walking in His Holy Light,
I will listen for His Voice,
Knowing He makes the Right Choice,
Why do you wonder at His Leading?
Christ is forever pleading,
He's the Potter, you are the clay,
Let Him mold you Day by Day

A Time

There is a time and there is a place, where we can see His Lovely Face,

Amid the stars and Heavenly light, where Jesus's Glory shines so bright,

O, look around and you will see, all of the joys He's planned for thee,

So step upon this Beautiful Place and partake of This Amazing Grace

Prayer

Prayer is powerful, dear and sweet, when we
bow at Jesus's feet,
He looks down and sees us there, just to
show us that He cares,
O how precious is His Love, that comes to
Fill us from Above,
Stay with me a little while, and we'll know
that we're His Child

Why Wonder?

If you will seek the Truth,
The Truth will set you Free,
If you will seek His Love,
It will shine down on thee,
Oh, why not Trust and Wait?
He is calling thee,
To make of thee His Vessel,
And you shall truly see,
It was in His Plan,
Long before you were,
To make of thee His Own,
And Fill you with His Love

The Arms of Jesus

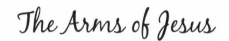

In the Arms of Jesus,
I shall not fret or fear,
For He is close beside me,
For He is ever near,
And though the trials come and go,
I'm safely in His Care,
For He's concerned about me,
And He is always there,
Oh, won't you come go with me?
To higher heights of Joy,
For He is God our Savior,
Of Him we can enjoy,
O, Thank You, Precious Savior,
For what you've done for me,
I will go tell Others,
Of the Beauty that I see

Blessed Jesus

Blessed Jesus, Lover of my soul,
Blessed Jesus, Blessed Jesus,
Blessed Jesus, Thou hast made me whole,
Blessed Jesus, Lover of my soul,
In the morning when I awake,
I am still with Thee,
And in the evening when I return,
Thou art close to me,
By the strength of Thy Power,
I am living every hour,
Blessed Jesus, Lover of my soul

Trust

Trust in Me, for I know the Way,
Trust in Me, for I'll lead you day by day,
Ever take Me by the hand,
Let Me lead you to the Land,
Trust in Me, though others may fail,
I Am thy God, and I shall prevail,
Dark and dreary may be the night,
Find in Me, thy Everlasting Light,
Yes, I know where thou must sod,
Fear not, My child, for I have trod,
Leaning on My Breast will keep you safe,
Trusting in Me, you will find much Grace,
I would bid you to please Be Still,
Resting in Me, My Perfect Will

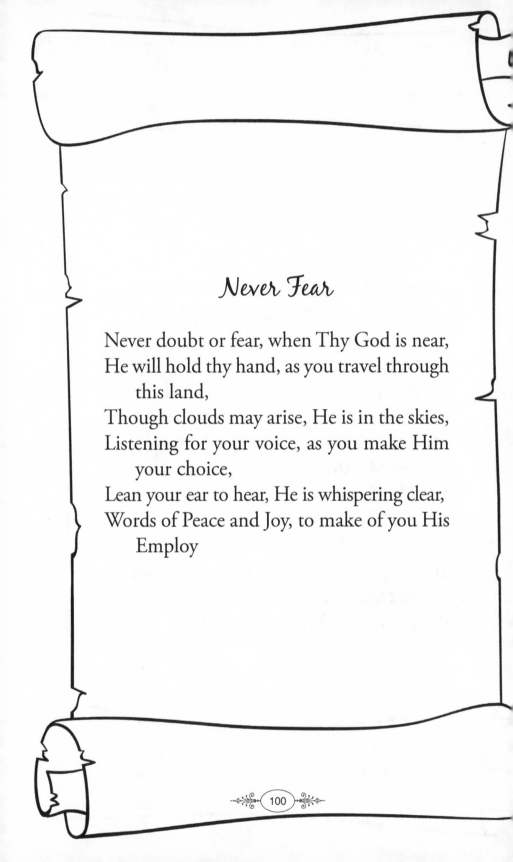

Never Fear

Never doubt or fear, when Thy God is near,
He will hold thy hand, as you travel through
    this land,
Though clouds may arise, He is in the skies,
Listening for your voice, as you make Him
    your choice,
Lean your ear to hear, He is whispering clear,
Words of Peace and Joy, to make of you His
    Employ

Nothing Is Impossibe

There's nothing that Jesus can't do,
He's Real if you let Him Be True,
Why doubt His Dear Word,
Please lean on the Lord,
There's nothing that Jesus can't do,
I know there are times,
When your Life doesn't Rhyme,
Please trust and obey,
And let Him have His Own Way,
There's Nothing that Jesus Can't Do,
Receive of His Best,
You can Stand the Test,
There's Nothing that Jesus Can't Do

Trusting

Trusting Jesus Day by Day,
Letting Him lead me along the way,
I have no need to fear the night,
For He is My Guiding Light,
The stars in heaven tell the story,
Of His matchless Grace and Glory,
Though I may stumble along the way,
He will surely help me, if I Pray,
Walking in the Sunlight of His Love,
Gives me Peace from above,
Don't you know He is Your King?
Lift your heart and let it sing

Chance

It is time to take a chance, on My Love from
    up Above,
You have sought most everywhere, to fulfill
    your needs and cares.
I am yet waiting for you to give me your heart,
And to meet with Hope at My own
    precious start,
You will be glad you did; I have what you
    need, only Hid,
I will reveal it to you if you will only see it
    through,
I know the way is tough, trust in Me, that's
    enough

A Prayer

I thought of you and said a prayer, because I
know You're always there,
To lead and guide along the way, Dear Lord
Jesus, you are my stay,
When I look around and see all that you
have done for me,
I cannot help but give you praise, for all
you've done through all my days

Grace

As clothes are a covering for the body, so
    His Grace
Is a covering to the Soul,
The Waters of Grace start at the root, going
    down deep,
Saturating, soaking at the very core of the
    Soul,
And moves upward until the Soul is
    completely alone
In Its waters; thriving and growing Day by
    Day
Until it Opens its arms and touches other
    souls,
As the Still Waters cover my Soul, O Lord,
So You have covered me

Belief

Though things may happen,
And you sometimes lose your way,
Trust in Jesus, for He is always there,
He will comfort and guide you, lead you in
    the way,
He is right beside you, to brighten your day,
Trust in Him anyway, though you can't see
    ahead,
He is your Best Friend and knows the road
    you take

The Rock

The Rock that holds true Christians Hearts
    is Jesus
He upholds and overshadows us with His
    Precious Love,
He will never let you fall, though the waters
    of Life may rise high,
Oh, look up Above, to the One you love,
He ever cares for thee, and will comfort you

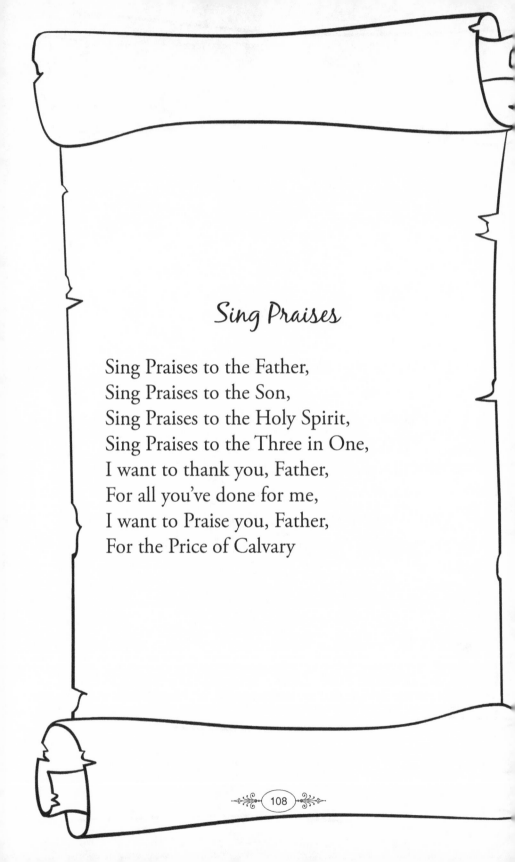

Sing Praises

Sing Praises to the Father,
Sing Praises to the Son,
Sing Praises to the Holy Spirit,
Sing Praises to the Three in One,
I want to thank you, Father,
For all you've done for me,
I want to Praise you, Father,
For the Price of Calvary

His Love

His Love is deeper than the sea,
Wider than you and me,
Oh, I love Him so,
Because He First Loved me,
Oh, bask in His Love,
It's from Above,
Believe me, It's True,
He Loves me and you

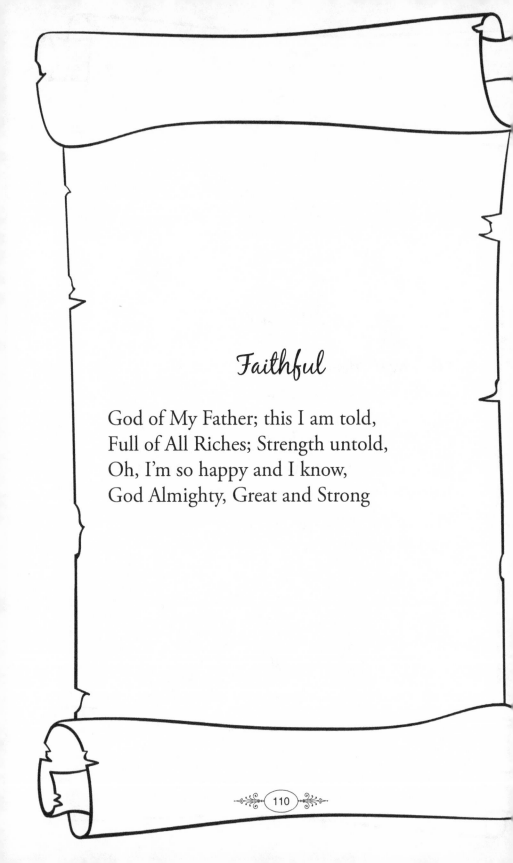

Faithful

God of My Father; this I am told,
Full of All Riches; Strength untold,
Oh, I'm so happy and I know,
God Almighty, Great and Strong

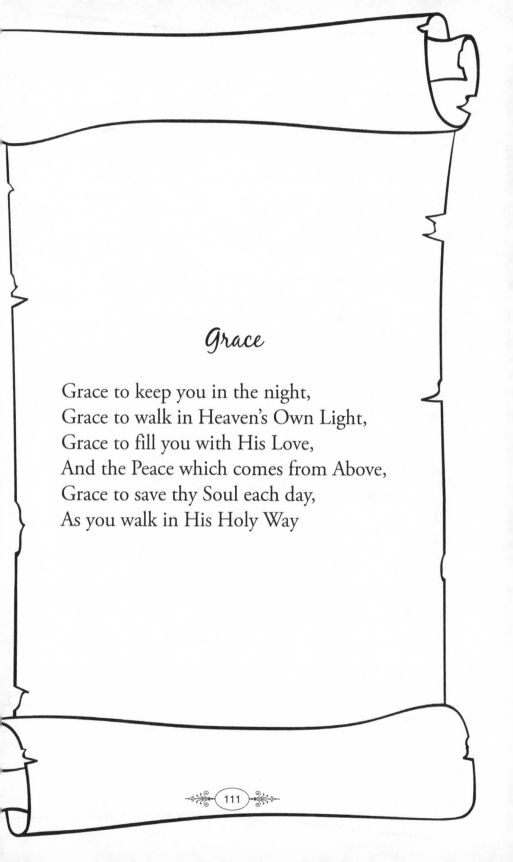

Grace

Grace to keep you in the night,
Grace to walk in Heaven's Own Light,
Grace to fill you with His Love,
And the Peace which comes from Above,
Grace to save thy Soul each day,
As you walk in His Holy Way

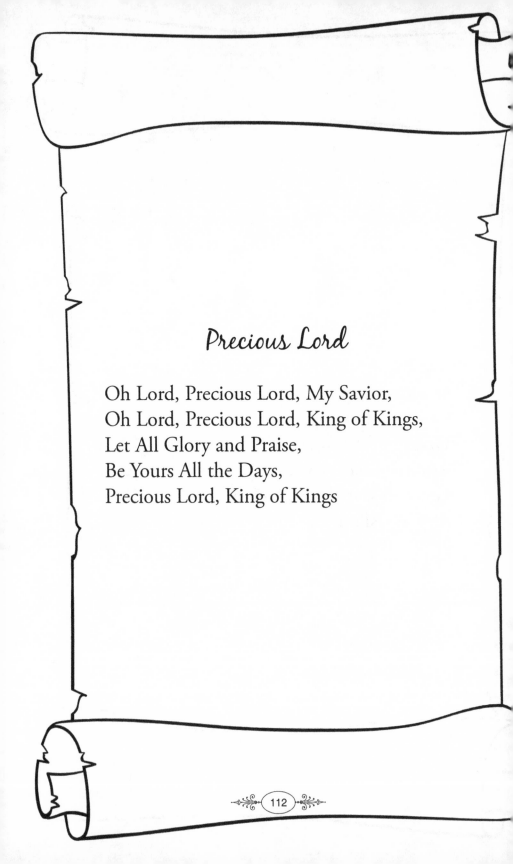

Precious Lord

Oh Lord, Precious Lord, My Savior,
Oh Lord, Precious Lord, King of Kings,
Let All Glory and Praise,
Be Yours All the Days,
Precious Lord, King of Kings

Fear Not

Don't fear, thy God is near,
Trusting in His Holy Hand,
Let Him lead you through this land,
He will keep you from All harm,
Guide you safely with His Mighty Arm,
Fear not what life may do,
God Will Take Good Care of You

Free

I once was bound, but Jesus set me free,
In His Love, He showed on Calvary,
I'm happy now, He cared for me,
For in His Blood, I am Truly Free,

Do Not Doubt

At any time, I Am yours and you are mine,
Within My Hand, is Grace Anew,
I will gladly, most gladly show it to you,
Please Rest here upon your bed,
Please lie still and rest your head,
Upon My Breast, seek Me till,
I come to you and fulfill,
All the joys you desire,
I have waiting in My Hand, this very hour,
Cease to struggle, until you are set free,
Free to love, and shout, and sing,
See, I give to you, My Everything

Heal Us

O, Comforting Spirit,
Heal us, we pray,
O Comforting Spirit,
Heal us today,
Thou hast healed us before,
We wait at Thy Door,
Never doubting Thy Power,
Please Heal us this hour

Your Love

Your love is Best,
It has always stood the Test,
Way back at Calvary,
Jesus is the One who died for me,
Waiting for me to see,
His Love has set me Free,
From Satan's power,
O, worship with me this hour

The Day

This could be the day, when your sins are
washed away,
When your life is made New, all because
Jesus Loves You,
O, look to God Above, only He can show
you His Love,
It is Christ, God sent to earth, because Of
Jesus's humble birth,
To save us from sin's power, and deliver us
in this hour
Please trust your life to Him alone, so that
you can have
a new Home
Come to Jesus now and say, only Jesus is the
Life, the Truth,
and the Only Way

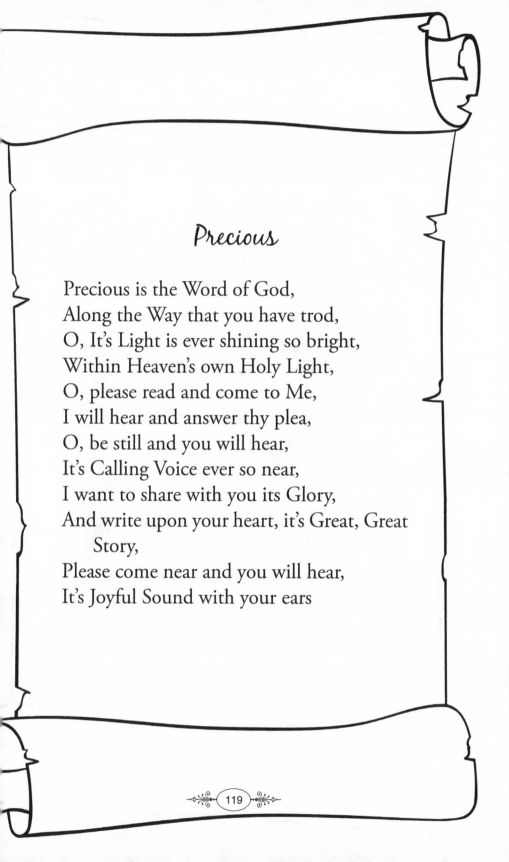

Precious

Precious is the Word of God,
Along the Way that you have trod,
O, It's Light is ever shining so bright,
Within Heaven's own Holy Light,
O, please read and come to Me,
I will hear and answer thy plea,
O, be still and you will hear,
It's Calling Voice ever so near,
I want to share with you its Glory,
And write upon your heart, it's Great, Great
    Story,
Please come near and you will hear,
It's Joyful Sound with your ears

Close

Come close to My Heart, and see,
All the blessings I have for thee,
I know sometimes it is hard to believe,
That I have chosen you to receive,
Keep your eyes looking up to Me,
I have what you need, don't lose your
    expectancy,
Build your hopes on things eternal,
I will always keep you from stumbling,
Way far up Above is My Love anew,
Waiting, yes, waiting to pour it upon you

Precious Father

Precious Father, Lord of Love,
Fill us with Thy Spirit from Above,
Hold us ever so close this hour,
Till we feel Thy Holy and Wondrous Power,
Lord, we kneel down and Pray,
Thank You for this Precious Day,
In it we feel Thy Love anew,
Bless your Holy Name for passing it through,
To us your children knowing not,
That through Jesus, your Son, this Great
    Salvation was bought,
With the Price of His Own Blood,
Now we know this Precious Love

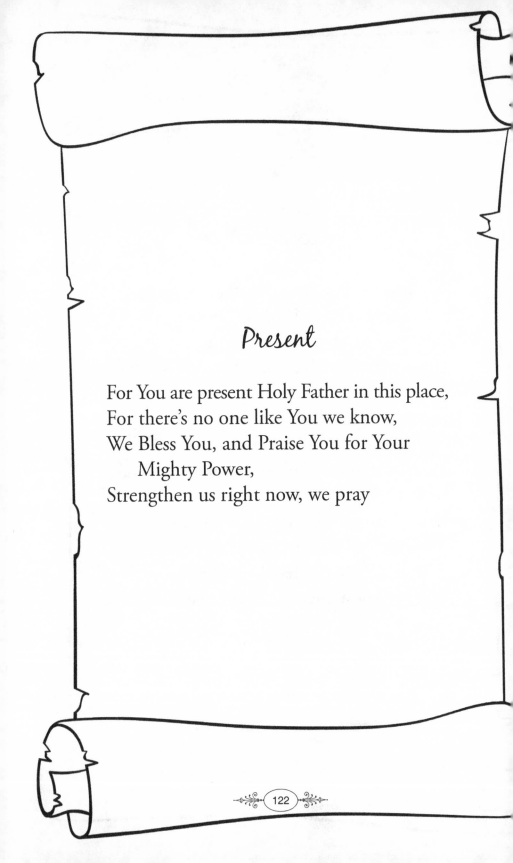

Present

For You are present Holy Father in this place,
For there's no one like You we know,
We Bless You, and Praise You for Your
    Mighty Power,
Strengthen us right now, we pray

Come

Come to waters so rich and sweet,
Come and kneel down at Jesus's feet,
He is waiting to meet you there,
And to hear your honest prayer,
O, listen to His Dear Voice,
And please make Him your only choice,
Come to the waters rich and sweet,
Stay please stay at Jesus's feet

When Jesus Comes

All things will become new, He it is, who
    died for you,
Way back on Calvary, to set the captives free,
The still of night becomes day, Jesus Christ
    is still The Way,
Won't you trust Him now? He's waiting for
    you this hour,
Don't give up yet, please come, though the
    Father Yet the Son,
His Way is best you know, come close and
    He will show,
All things are in His hands, your very life
    He commands,
Please look up, and you will see, He has
    come to set you free

He Is

He will never change all the plans He has
for you,
He will fulfill and arrange according to His
Perfect Will,
Please be still and wait, He is standing at
the Gate,
Open your heart and you will see all the
Plans He has for thee

Stretch Out

Stretch out on His Word, it is easy to be Heard,
Open up your eyes and see, it is only as you
  Believe,
Please trust in Him Today and let Him have
  His Precious Way,
Don't continue to doubt, only He can help
  you out,
His Word came from Up Above, please
  believe His every Word,
He wants to bring you close, so that you'll
  know He is The Most,
Place your Life into His Hands, on His
  Holy Word,
You can always stand,
No matter what the Test, Jesus Christ, God's
  Son is and
Always Will Be the Best

Thy Word

Thy Word is a Light unto my soul,
It Lifts me up,
It Heals me when I am sick,
It Feeds me when I am hungry,
It is Water to me, when I am thirsty,
It Comforts me in the night,
It Talks with me in the day,
It Keeps me when I lie down,
It Awakens me every morning,
It is My Constant Companion

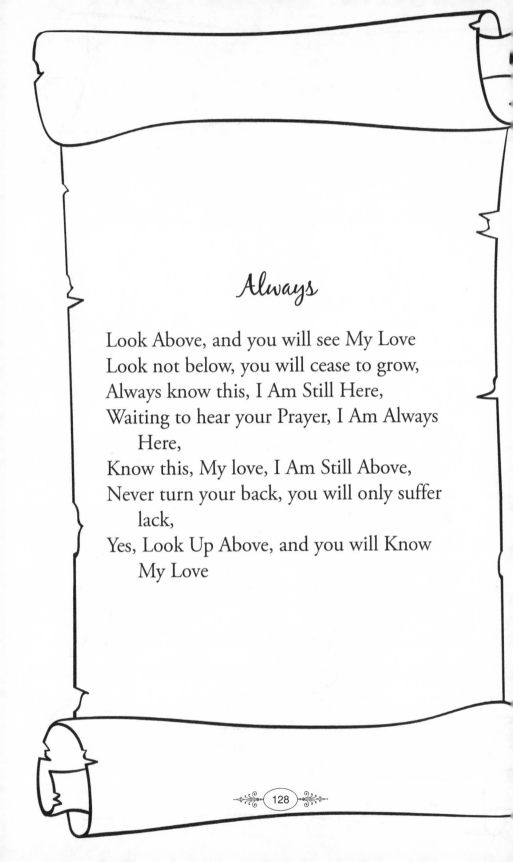

Always

Look Above, and you will see My Love
Look not below, you will cease to grow,
Always know this, I Am Still Here,
Waiting to hear your Prayer, I Am Always
    Here,
Know this, My love, I Am Still Above,
Never turn your back, you will only suffer
    lack,
Yes, Look Up Above, and you will Know
    My Love

Look

The clouds are rolled away,
It is the Dawning of a Bright New Day,
Look ahead, and not back,
It will only increase your lack,
I have come to set you free,
Turn your eyes and look to Me,
Yes, I know what lies ahead,
Let Me be your Fear and Dread,
Look not back over what could have been,
I Am He who knows All things,
Look ahead and be blessed,
You are made able to stand the test,
I have been with you before,
Do not seek to close the Door,
Let Me set you totally free,
Then you'll have all you need,
To keep Praising Me, Look Up!

I Wish You

Blessings ahead all of your days,
Plans anew throughout your stay,
Rain to wash away your tears,
Sun to dry up any trouble near,
Trust to see what I can do,
Blessings ahead with Brightness for you

Stone

There is a Stone, Precious and Sure,
There is a Stone, we know Endures
Soft and Bright, in its Light,
We find Peace and Joy forever more,
O, come and see, and you will be,
Strong and Sure, and forever endure

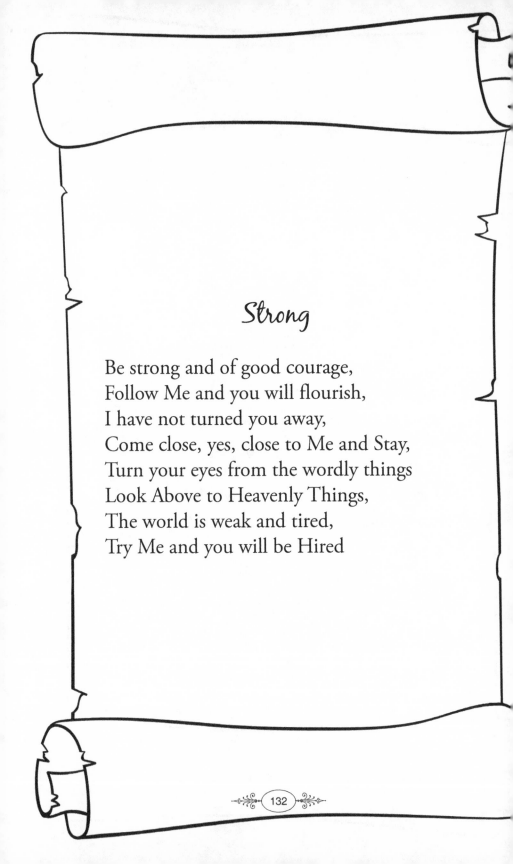

Strong

Be strong and of good courage,
Follow Me and you will flourish,
I have not turned you away,
Come close, yes, close to Me and Stay,
Turn your eyes from the wordly things
Look Above to Heavenly Things,
The world is weak and tired,
Try Me and you will be Hired

Rely

Rely on Me, I Paid the Cost,
Share with others that are lost,
Take what I have given to thee,
Trust Me Now and you will be free,
Free to do My Will at any cost,
So that you won't suffer loss,
Yes, Yes, I Am the Way,
I will lead and guide you from day to day

The Lord

The Lord is on my side,
I will not fret nor fear,
For He will stay close beside me,
For He is ever near,
Though storm clouds gather around me,
Sometime thick and dark,
He comes to give me sunshine,
Within my very heart,
And so I can face tomorrow,
Whatever may come or go,
I have put my trust in Jesus,
Because He loves me so,
You too can have this assurance,

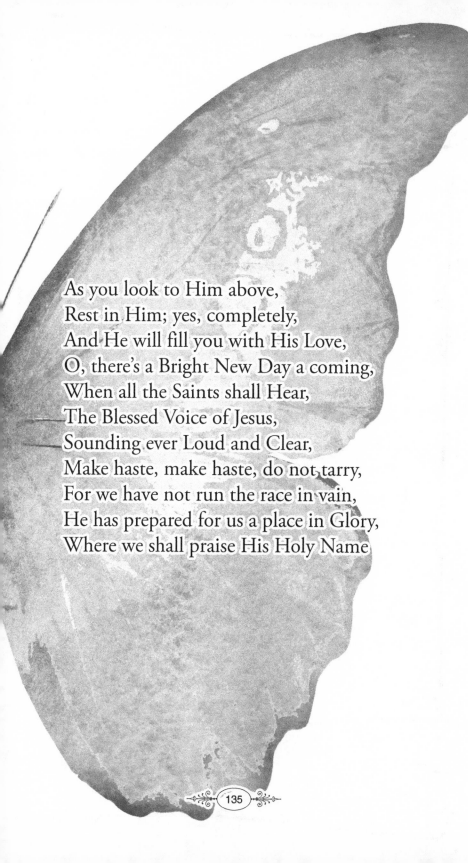

As you look to Him above,
Rest in Him; yes, completely,
And He will fill you with His Love,
O, there's a Bright New Day a coming,
When all the Saints shall Hear,
The Blessed Voice of Jesus,
Sounding ever Loud and Clear,
Make haste, make haste, do not tarry,
For we have not run the race in vain,
He has prepared for us a place in Glory,
Where we shall praise His Holy Name

Near

I Am Here, I'm Ever so Near,
Look up in the sky, for I dwell on High,
Cast your cares on Me, For I can See,
All that concerns you, also concerns Me,
Hope, yes, hope to see, I Am always near you,
And I will set you Free

Trust

Trust the way that I have given thee,
Trust the way that I have trod,
Lo, there is a path before thee,
Look to me, for I Am Thy God,
There are those that go before thee,
There are those that I have called,
Rejoice in Me, for I Am with thee,
Rejoice in Me, for I Am Thy God

Teach

You can only teach what you have been
    taught,
All the works of old, In God has been
    wrought,
Through Wisdom, Knowledge, and
    Understanding too,
This precious Gift is also given to you,
You can help others know the Way,
Only as you share and teach them what
    God has said

Best

Hope for the Best, this is the Test,
Never doubt or fear, for Jesus thy Savior is
    near,
Troubles and trials must come
Jesus can take you through,
Jesus, God's only Son,
He is ever Faithful and True,
Blossoms are near, be of Good Cheer,
Always hope for the Best

Carry

Carry on a little while longer,
I Am Able to make thee stronger,
Along life's path you will see,
It is I, It is Me,
Lift your eyes up above,
Come and see, Taste of My Love,
It was for you, that I came to earth,
Yes, was through My Humble birth,
To show you only that I Care,
Through this you will be able to bear

May

May you be blessed with sunshine, In your
very heart,

May you be blessed with goodness, Yes, on
every start,

May your life hold the key, So that you can be,

All that was planned before because I Am
that Everlasting Door,

Through Me, you can see, everything in
this whole wide world,

That you were purposed to Be

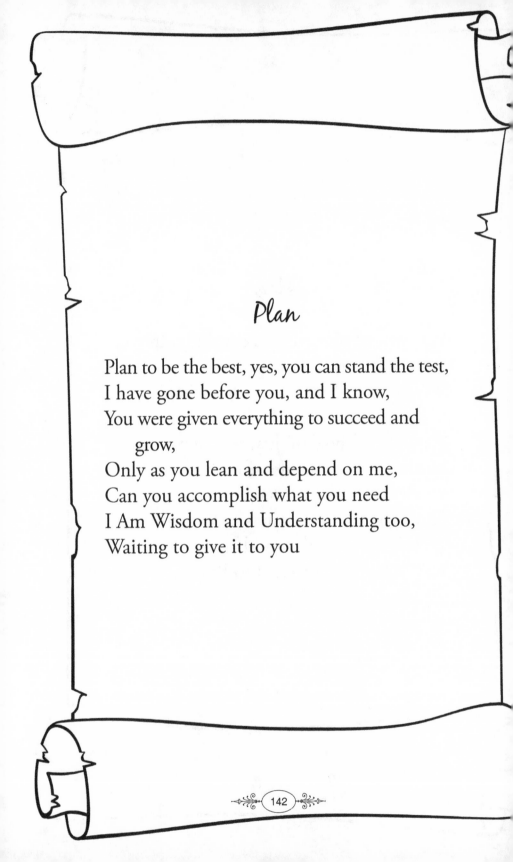

Plan

Plan to be the best, yes, you can stand the test,
I have gone before you, and I know,
You were given everything to succeed and
 grow,
Only as you lean and depend on me,
Can you accomplish what you need
I Am Wisdom and Understanding too,
Waiting to give it to you

Touch

Touch the Hem of My Garment, and you
  shall be Saved,
Touch the Hem of My Garment, and you
  shall be Healed,
I Am thy Savior from up above, let me
  Always fill you with My Love
Is there anything that you need?
Come ever so close to Me,
For I Am He, who knows everything about
  you,
Let Me fill your soul, and you will know
  that I Am True

Shepherd

I Am your Shepherd, you are My child,
I Am your Shepherd, always Lowly, Meek,
and Mild,
Look to Me for all you need, I Am Jesus, the
Holy Seed,
I will lead you in Paths anew, when you
realize I Am True,
Do Not run ahead, wait for me, I know
what you need,
And I will Lead

Relax

Relax in My Arms,
I Am the Way,
Relax in My Arms,
I'm here to stay,
I've told you before,
I Am the Door,
Look up and Be Still,
This is My Perfect Will

Return

Where have you Gone? I Have looked for you,
Longing to continue holding you close
    beside me,
Teaching, showing, and revealing of Myself
    to you,
Do you choose to stay away from the Light
    of Life?
That awaits to fill your heart with
    overflowing joy,
Peace, and abundance of everything you
    will ever
Need in this life, and the Life to come?

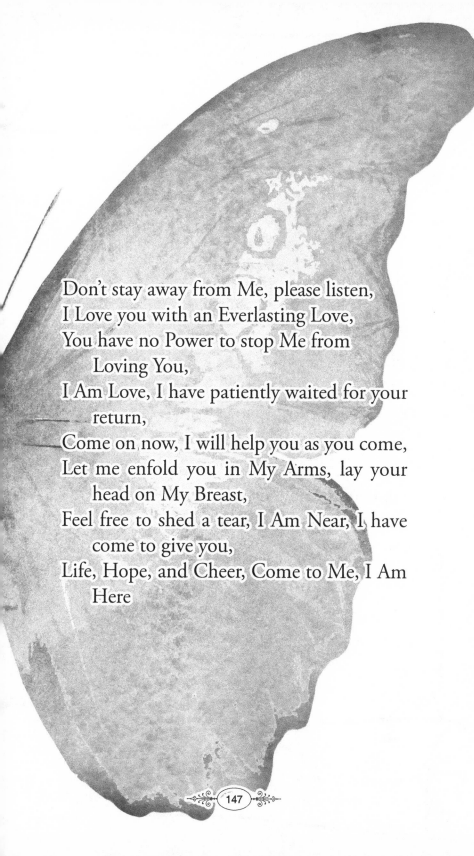

Don't stay away from Me, please listen,
I Love you with an Everlasting Love,
You have no Power to stop Me from
    Loving You,
I Am Love, I have patiently waited for your
    return,
Come on now, I will help you as you come,
Let me enfold you in My Arms, lay your
    head on My Breast,
Feel free to shed a tear, I Am Near, I have
    come to give you,
Life, Hope, and Cheer, Come to Me, I Am
    Here

Trust Him

There's Rain at the end of the Highway,
There's Rain at the end of the Road,
Just hold on a little bit longer,
And He will carry your load,
So trust Him and come on farther,
He knows what you're going through,
Yes, Believe in God your Savior,
For He is the one who cares for you

The Morning Has Come

It's going to be a bright new day,
Can you hear the birds singing?
As they fly and go about their way,
Look Up, Look Up to the Heavens,
God's handiwork is brand-New today,
He's the One that made us,
Surely, He'll show us His Way

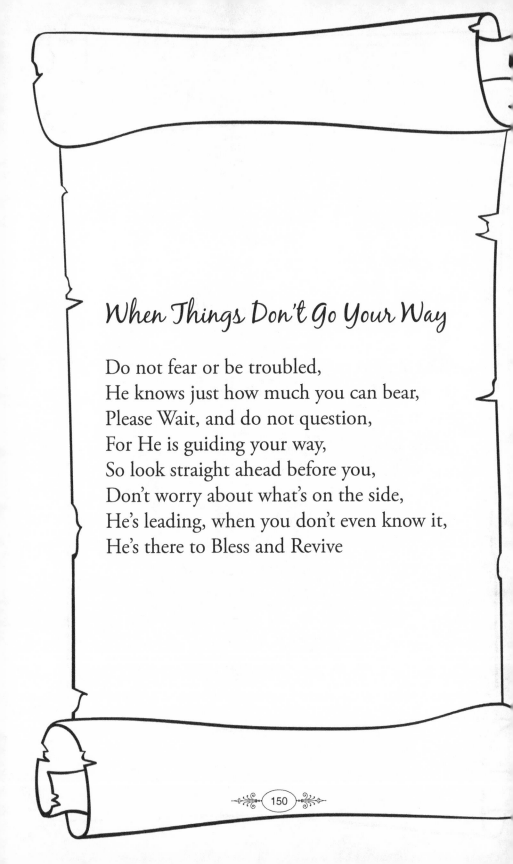

When Things Don't Go Your Way

Do not fear or be troubled,
He knows just how much you can bear,
Please Wait, and do not question,
For He is guiding your way,
So look straight ahead before you,
Don't worry about what's on the side,
He's leading, when you don't even know it,
He's there to Bless and Revive

Lessons He Teaches

May seem New or Strange,
There you must be still,
And Praise His Holy Name,
He Knows what's before you,
On the Left hand and the Right,
He wants you to grow and prosper,
In His Blessed and Holy Sight
You are His Son, He knows you,
He made you Bright and Smart
Lean on Him, Come closer,
He knows the End from the Start

Believe Him!

When He says I Love You,
When He tells you I Care,
When He says I'll provide for you,
When He tells others to share,
So don't try to hide your burden,
Or shift your load to the side,
He's standing right beside you,
Waiting to be your Guide,
Stop trusting in yourself,
He knows all your needs,
Believe Christ, your Savior,
For to you alone He pleads

I See You

I see you where you stand,
Please come and take My Hand,
Believe Me Only; Don't be Lonely,
I will lead you to that blessed Promised
    Land,
You shall no more fear, for I Am Always
    near,
Come unto Me And Rest,
And you shall Know that I Am The Best

Alone

Alone with Jesus along the way,
Alone with Jesus is My Stay,
He walks beside me, and I know,
He alone always causes me to grow,
Up and Up, Higher and Higher,
Is His Love and Mighty Power

He Knows You

Oh, you may try to hide or wander,
Far from the Hand of God,
When you fall or falter,
Not knowing the path you trod,
Continuing in your own darkness,
Not seeking the Light from above,
Do not stray any longer,
He longs to hold you near,
Come back to Me, My Son or Daughter,
I Am Come to give you Cheer

Bright

There's a land so bright,
In Heaven's own light,
Please come and share,
And know that I Care,
I have come to thee,
Please come and see,
It was created for you,
To enjoy it and through,
Heaven's own Precious Gates,
It is a glad and joyous Place,
There's no weight or care,
For Jesus Himself is There,
Oh, wait right here,
And come on near,
You'll see His Face,
In this Beautiful Great Place,
He wants to meet you There,
And It is where,
You can come Home,
And never again be alone,
Oh, Taste and See,
Jesus waits for thee

Look Down

Lord, look down on your people,
Lord, look down with Grace,
Lord, look down on your people,
Help us to behold your Face.
For we have sinned and turned from thee,
O, help us, Lord, to hear Thy plea,
As the shadows come,
And the darkness appears,
Lord, please help us,
Please come near,
Thank you for your Precious Grace,
Help us, Lord, as we seek your Face,
We are Still before you now,
Please help us, Lord, for you know how,
Help us to Return to thee,
This is our earnest plea,
As we feel your tender Rod,
Help us to know that you Alone are God

Morning

The dawn of morning is near,
Bringing hopes of cheer,
A bright promise of a new day,
Always takes your cares away,
Think of Me, and take a sigh,
I Am near you, and here is why,
I have come to give you Joy,
With the rising of each new day,
I am near you especially, Early in The Morning

How Great Is Thy Love!

How Great is Thy Love!
It came from Above.
Through Jesus, My Savior,
And His Holy Spirit,
In the Form of a Dove,
Won't you let Him Enclose you,
There's nothing to fear,
For He will gently hold you,
And keep you ever so near,
How great is His Goodness!
In All that He Does,
Look up and behold Him
In the Beautiful Heavens Above.
O, Reach out and Touch Him,
Through Hearing His Word,
He ever wants to Tell You,
How Great Is His LOVE!

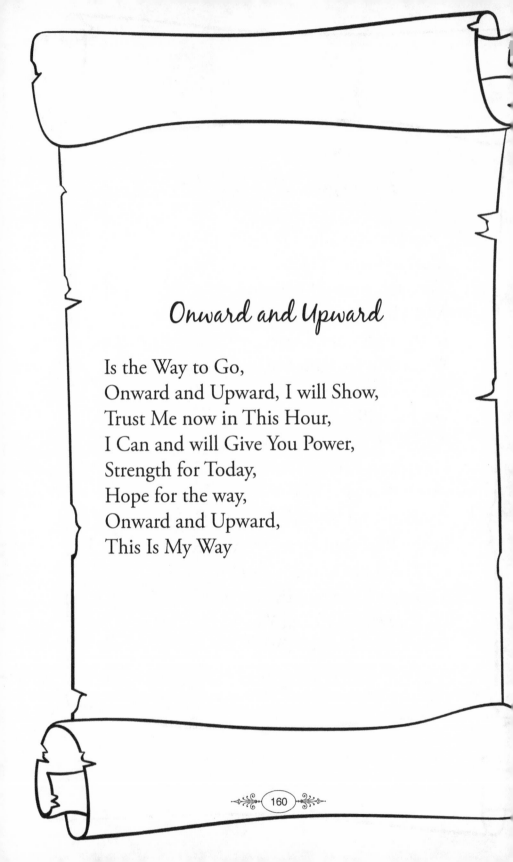

Onward and Upward

Is the Way to Go,
Onward and Upward, I will Show,
Trust Me now in This Hour,
I Can and will Give You Power,
Strength for Today,
Hope for the way,
Onward and Upward,
This Is My Way

Pray

For the Hour Is late,
Behold, I Stand at The Gate,
Of the Hearts of Women and Men,
To give All Everlasting Joy within
Pray for them; children and young people too,
To be saved from the fate,
That is coming soon,
I Am Not willing that any should perish,
But that all be Saved and ever flourish,
Don't look at things at hand,
I Am All they will Ever need,
And I Am Here Always to Stand,
Open your Mouth and Tell them,
I will give you what to Say,
Stay close to Me and you will,
Warn Them while it is Day

Precious Love

O, How Sweet is His Love,
Given to us from Up Above, God Is Love,
  you see,
It is promised to you and to me,
Open your heart wide to receive,
Of His Love and Victory, Over sin's power
  and loss,
God gave His Dear Son to Pay the Cost,
His Love is Forever Free, Paid For us at
  Calvary,
O, won't you seek His Love
It is Free to all who Come

Praise

Praise Me Now for All I've Done
I Am Jesus Christ, God's Son,
Look at Me, and not at you,
I Am He that will ever choose,
All the Ways that you should go,
Look to Me and you will know,
I Am Here to Give you Peace,
Trust Me Now and know Sweet Release

Dwell

Come and dwell with Me this hour,
I want to give you what you need, More
    Power,
I still dwell up Above,
Please come and Taste of My Love,
I know the hour is short,
Let Me Show you, My Blessed Part,
Seek to know Me from within,
In My Realm are Blessings Hid,
Open up your heart to receive My Love,
I will Bless and Keep you from Above,
Let go completely of the past,
I Am Love, and I Shall Last

The Cross

The Cross where Jesus died,
His Love there, Sill Abides,
It was for me, you know,
His Broken Heart did show,
The Love for All Mankind,
Jesus, so Pure and yet also Divine,
His Life in the Water and Blood,
Flowed from His Side in Love,
The Centurion knew for Sure,
That Jesus, The Son of God, Was Pure,
He died that we might Live,
Praise God! For Jesus Is Real!

Rise

Rise and Shine, I Am Thine,
I Care for thee, Come and See,
What's in Store, I Am the Door,
I Died for thee, To Set you Free,
Please Come Near, You Are Dear
I Am your Guide, where you can Hide,
From All your fears, for I Am Near,
Seek Me Until, you are Completely Filled

I Love You

I Love You, can't you see?
I have come to set you free,
From the Power of sin and death,
I know you can stand the test,
Life brings Solace, Peace, and Joy
I have come to bring you even more,
There is Healing, In My Wings,
Enough to make your very Heart sing,
I Am waiting at the Door,
I Am Here to give you so much more,
Sing, O Rejoice, Sing to Me,
I Have Come, To Set You Free

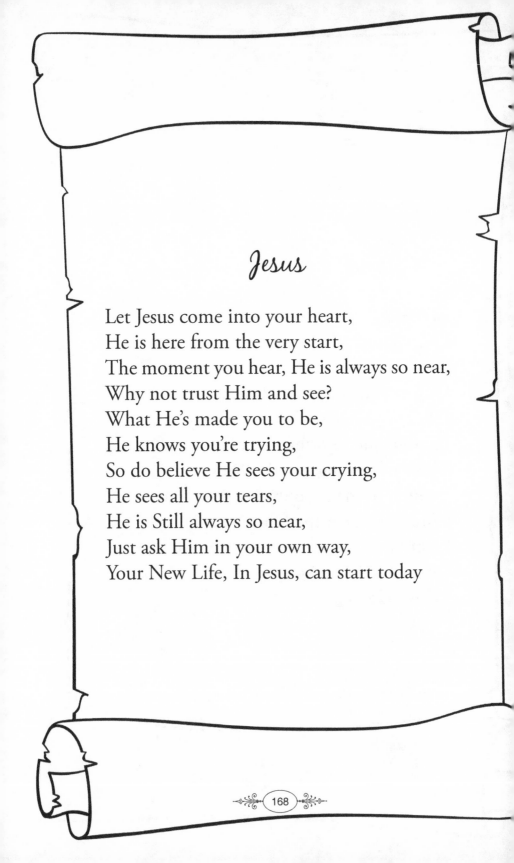

Jesus

Let Jesus come into your heart,
He is here from the very start,
The moment you hear, He is always so near,
Why not trust Him and see?
What He's made you to be,
He knows you're trying,
So do believe He sees your crying,
He sees all your tears,
He is Still always so near,
Just ask Him in your own way,
Your New Life, In Jesus, can start today

Look

Look to Me and see,
It is I that have Glorified thee,
I have put you in this place,
And you shall run this race,
Look ahead and you will see,
All that I will give unto thee,
Though the road gets rough and dreary,
You shall not at all grow weary,
Yes, you have come this far,
Look ahead to Me, I am Your Star

Sitting

Sitting at the feet of Jesus,
There is room for you and me,
Sitting at the feet of Jesus,
Oh, please come near, and you will see,
There is much to hear and learn,
Oh, Be Careful not to spurn,
He wants you to know until,
There will be no doubt that He Is Real,
Do not hasten to go away,
Words of Wisdom will Brighten your day,
Oh, Please Taste and See,
That God is good,
In His Presence you know you should

You Alone

You alone who died on the Cross,
And gave your Life and Grace to atone,
You alone who Suffered for me,
So that I could have a Life Full and Free,
O, thank you, Father, way up Above,
For giving your Son and His Sweet Love

Walk

Walk toward Me, I know what's Best,
Walk toward Me, you can stand the Test,
Look not to the left nor to the right,
I Am beside you, see My Light,
Onward and upward you may go,
I Am Thy God, and I will show,
All My Purpose for you to see,
I Am He that made thee,
Look up, Look up, and see My Light,
I Am the Way, The Truth shining Bright

Trust

Though things may happen,
And you sometimes lose your way,
Trust in Jesus, for He is Always there,
He will Comfort and Guide you,
Lead you in the Way,
He is right beside you,
To Brighten you Day,
Trust in Him anyway,
Though you can't see ahead,
He is your Best Friend,
And knows the Road you take

Be Thankful

For the Rain, For the Pain,
God Is Near, and He will Always Hear,
He knows, and He provides all the things,
We need to help us to succeed,
He knows Best and will help us stand every
single Test,
Look to God Up Above, and Be Thankful
for His Love

Grow

You can grow, yes, indeed you can,
If you put your hand in the Master's Hand,
He knows all about you, you know,
Only He can cause you to grow,
You'll be surprised when you see how far
    you've come,
Only to know you've just begun,
He is the Only Way, trust Him Now,
Then you will confidently know How

Step Out

On to Nothing, that is what Faith is all about,
You don't See it, yet you Believe It,
Only God can help you out,
Look above to the One who Loves you,
He's ever by Your Side,
Lift up your Hands and Praise Him,
He Alone will be your Guide

Step Into

Step into the Light,
God's own Heavenly Light,
There is Peace and Joy,
As you see His employ,
There is Light anew,
Always waiting for you,
As you seek His Face,
You will have much Grace,
Never look back,
There is only lack,
Look ahead to God,
His Way you can trod,
You can go through,
He is waiting for you,
Never doubt or give up,
Christ Jesus Alone can fill your Cup

Dearest Father

Dearest Father Up Above, fill us with thy
  Dear Sweet Love,
Until we overflow so that others can grow,
As we look away up High, at the Beautiful
  deep blue sky,
We know that You love us so, and you want
  us to continue to grow,
So come now and stay, until we see the Light
  of Day,
We cannot hide because You are our Guide,
Fill us, we pray, and ever Lead us in Thy Way

Day

The Breaking of Day is the Beginning of Life,
Where you will see no Strife,
For It is Peaceful, Calm, and Sure,
Where you shall evermore endure,
There is up above so High,
God's Word's written in the Sky,
Where Angels dwell and long to see,
His inheritance forever in Us to Be,
O, See His Face Above,
Bending over us In Love,
You can have His Peace anew,
As you let Him draw closer to you,
O, Let this Power from Above,
Fill you with His Precious Love

Rest a While

Rest a while and see the Goodness of God,
Rest a while and see the Path that He has trod,
Rest a while, there is Time yet,
To seek His Peace and Happiness,
Rest a while and Praise His Name,
Rest a while He is Ever the Same

Turn

To Me, and see My Light,
I Am Shining ever So Bright,
I came to give you, Life Anew,
Trust Me Now to bring it to you,
Don't be bound by what others may say,
I Am God, I made The Day,
Don't give up and slip away,
Strength in Me is your Way,
Come a little closer now,
I will gladly show you How

Friends

We meet people along the way,
And find them interesting, they make our day,
As time goes on, they are like a sturdy tree,
We can lean against and feel so free,
Sometimes we laugh, sometimes we cry,
Sharing each other's thoughts, as time goes by,
Like shining jewels, they sparkle when we
    meet,
Just sharing each other's time ever so sweet,
Don't ever forget or leave them alone,
Only for a short time are they our own,
God loves and cares for each one of us as
    Friends,
If we only believe and trust Him until the end

Until

You do the things I've asked you to, you
    won't have Peace,
You forgive others their mistakes, you won't
    have Peace,
You rely on Me for your everything, you
    won't have Peace,
You love yourself, you won't have Peace,
Ask, Seek, Knock continuously, then you'll
    have Peace

Chosen

Chosen before the World begun,
Chosen to be God's only Dear Son,
Prepared on High with God's own Love,
Chosen to be with The Holy Dove,
I Am He who goes before thee,
Follow the Path that I have trod,
Yes, Yes, My Name is Jesus Christ,
I Am the Holy One that dwells on High,
Walk before Me and ever be True,
There is much work before thee,
Works that only you can do,
Call upon Me, for I Am Near,
I only want to Bless and keep you,
For you are Mine, and I call you Dear

Stay

Though your way may be dark and slippery,
Jesus Christ is your Guide and Stay,
Please trust Him with your heart,
He knows every part,
Stay within His Will,
Your heart's desire, He will fulfill,
Lean your weary head upon His Breast,
He knows every single test,
Though you know not how to cry,
Jesus Christ is standing by,
Keep on looking up,
He is ready and willing to fill your cup

Mama

There is no Prayer, like a Mother's Prayer,
There is no Voice, like a Mother's Voice,
There is no Song, like a Mother's Song,
There are no Words, like a Mother's Words,
There is no Touch, like a Mother's Touch,
There is no Strength, like a Mother's
    Strength,
There is no Wisdom, like a Mother's
    Wisdom,
There is no Heart, like a Mother's Heart,
There is no Kiss, like a Mother's Kiss,
There is no Comfort, like a Mother's
    Comfort,
There is no Love, like a Mother's Love

About the Author

My name is Cathy Peters Gilot, married to Pierre T. Gilot. I come from a large family of ten children, of whom I am third in line. The scriptures used in the poems and also the title of the book are from the King James Bible. As early as the third grade, my teacher asked the students what they wanted to be when they grew up. I hadn't given it much thought and said I wanted to be a writer. As the years passed by, it was not until 1980 that God brought the gift in me to fruition, and I began to write a few poems. I had not realized the precious value of the gift. I did not tell or show them to anyone. By 2016, the gift resurfaced by God's Holy Spirit. I was awakened in the very early hours of the morning to write what was being given to me. I wrote these in my journal until I filled most of it. I was urged to share these precious poems with others. Also God gave to me personalized poems for certain people which were for them only. I pray that everyone in need of hope, peace, comfort, joy, etc., will be blessed by these poems.